D0761912

Hillsboro Public Library
Hillsboro, OR
A member of Washington County
COOPERATIVE LIBRARY SERVICES

Discovering Dinosaurs

PREHISTORIC CREATURES OF THE SEA AND SKIES

Consulting Editor: Carl Mehling

Skyview Books™
an imprint of
WINDMILL BOOKS™
New York

Published in 2010 by Windmill Books, LLC
303 Park Avenue South, Suite # 1280, New York, NY 10010-3657

Copyright © 2010 Amber Books Ltd
Adaptations to North American Edition © 2010 Windmill Books

All rights reserved. No part of this book may be reproduced in any form without permission in writing from the publisher, except by a reviewer.

CREDITS:
Consulting Editor: Carl Mehling
Designer: Graham Beehag

Publisher Cataloging in Publication

Prehistoric creatures of the sea and skies / consulting editor, Carl Mehling.
p. cm. – (Discovering dinosaurs)
Summary: With the help of fossil evidence this book provides physical descriptions of twenty-five prehistoric animals that either flew or lived in the ocean.—Contents: Henodus—Nanchangosaurus—Nothosaurus—Shonisaurus—Dimorphodon—Liopleurodon—Archaeopteryx—Ophthalmosaurus—Dsungaripterus—Tapejara—Tropeognathus—Kronosaurus—Pterodaustro—Elasmosaurus—Xiphactinus—Tylosaurus—Quetzalcoatlus—Libonectes (Elasmosaur)—Mosasaur—Pteranodon—Hesperornis—Mammalodon—Basilosaurus—Argentavis—Carcharocles (Megalodon).
ISBN 978-1-60754-773-0. – ISBN 978-1-60754-781-5 (pbk.)
ISBN 978-1-60754-855-3 (6-pack)
33614057735473
1. Birds, Fossil—Juvenile literature   2. Marine animals, Fossil—Juvenile literature   [1. Birds, Fossil   2. Marine animals, Fossil   3. Prehistoric animals]
I. Mehling, Carl   II. Series
560—dc22

Printed in the United States

CPSIA Compliance Information: Batch #BW10W: For further information contact Windmill Books, New York, New York at 1-866-478-0556.

CONTENTS

Introduction

Imagining what our world was like in the distant past is a lot like being a detective. There were no cameras around, and there were no humans writing history books. In many cases, fossils are all that remain of animals who have been extinct for millions of years.

Fossils are the starting point that scientists use to make educated guesses about what life was like in prehistoric times. And while fossils are important, even the best fossil can't tell the whole story. If snakes were extinct, and all we had left were their bones, would anyone guess that they could snatch bats from the air in pitch-black caves? Probably not, but there is a Cuban species of snake that can do just that. Looking at a human skeleton wouldn't tell you how many friends that person had, or what their favorite color was. Likewise, fossils can give us an idea of how an animal moved and what kind of food it ate, but they can't tell us everything about an animal's behavior or what life was like for them.

Our knowledge of prehistoric life is constantly changing to fit the new evidence we have. While we may never know everything, the important thing is that we continue to learn and discover. Learning about the history of life on Earth, and trying to piece together the puzzle of the dinosaurs, can help us understand more about our past and future.

Henodus

• **ORDER** • Placodontia • **FAMILY** • Henodontidae • **GENUS & SPECIES** • *Henodus chelyops*

VITAL STATISTICS

FOSSIL LOCATION	Germany
DIET	Shellfish
PRONUNCIATION	hen-O-dus
WEIGHT	Unknown
LENGTH	3 ft (1 m)
HEIGHT	Unknown
MEANING OF NAME	"Single tooth" because it was first thought to have only one tooth on each side of its skull

WHERE IN THE WORLD?

Currently, the only *Henodus* fossils have been dug up in Tübingen, Germany. But placodont fossils have turned up in other parts of Europe as well as in the Middle East and North Africa.

If you saw *Henodus* crawling along the floor of a lagoon you might think it was a turtle, but it was only a distant cousin with similar habits.

TEETH
Henodus had two teeth, one on each side of its mouth toward the back. But a new specimen shows tiny teeth at the front of the jaws, too. The lower jaws were completely toothless.

FOSSIL EVIDENCE

Henodus was a placodont of the Late Triassic Period. It is known from several fossils, including a well-preserved, complete, skeleton. Placodonts were a mixed group of aquatic reptiles of the Triassic. Some placodonts developed a body form similar to today's marine iguana, while others developed armor and became turtle-like. Some scientists think that the long-tailed, armored types behaved like stingrays. From studying fossils, scientists think that placodonts were designed to spend more time in water than on land.

HOW BIG IS IT?

PREHISTORIC ANIMAL

TRIASSIC

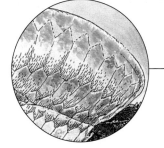

SHELL
The protective shell of *Henodus* was made up of tightly packed bony plates connected to the ribs (like a turtle's shell). But, unlike turtles, the limb girdles (supports) stayed outside of the rib cage.

TIMELINE (millions of years ago)

| 540 | 505 | 438 | 408 | 360 | 280 | 248 | 208 | 146 | 65 | 1.8 to today |

Nanchangosaurus

• ORDER • Ichthyosauria • FAMILY • Nanchangosauridae • GENUS & SPECIES • *Nanchangosaurus sur*

VITAL STATISTICS

FOSSIL LOCATION	China
DIET	Carnivorous
PRONUNCIATION	Nan-CHANG-oh-SAWR-us
WEIGHT	Unknown
LENGTH	3 ft (1 m)
HEIGHT	Unknown
MEANING OF NAME	"Nanchang lizard" after the part of China where it was discovered

This marine reptile seems to have been a bit "behind the times." This tetrapod had seven toes. Scientists find this strange because it lived 100 million years after relatives who had developed limbs with five, instead of seven, toes.

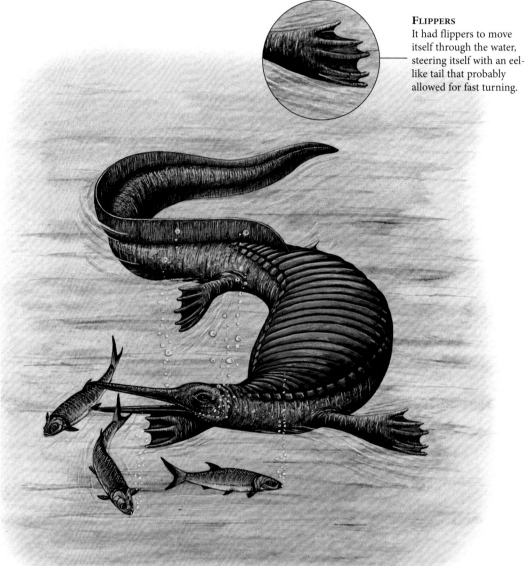

FLIPPERS
It had flippers to move itself through the water, steering itself with an eel-like tail that probably allowed for fast turning.

EYES
The head features large eyes, suggesting good eyesight and a long toothless snout for snapping up its marine diet.

FOSSIL EVIDENCE

It is a bit of a mystery why this reptile had seven digits on its front limbs and six on its hind limbs. Early four-legged animals *Ichthyostega* and *Acanthostega* had seven or eight digits on each limb, but their descendants (relatives who came later) lost them as they evolved. The *Nanchangosaurus*'s extra digits may have made it a better swimmer. It is possible that such reptiles form the "missing link" between aquatic ichthyosaurs and their land-based archosaur ancestors.

PREHISTORIC ANIMAL

TRIASSIC

HOW BIG IS IT?

WHERE IN THE WORLD?

The only remains have been found in the Jiangxi province of southern China.

TIMELINE (millions of years ago)

540	505	438	408	360	280	248	208	146	65	1.8 to today

Nothosaurus

VITAL STATISTICS

FOSSIL LOCATION	Europe, Middle East, Asia, and North Africa
DIET	Fish and sea creatures
PRONUNCIATION	no-thoh-SAWR-us
WEIGHT	Unknown
LENGTH	10 ft (3 m)
HEIGHT	Unknown
MEANING OF NAME	"False lizard," since it only looked like a lizard

FOSSIL EVIDENCE

Nothosaurus was a reptile with a lifestyle kind of like a modern seal. It would probably hunt in shallow tropical seas, moving its sleek body toward schools of fish before pouncing with its teeth-lined jaw. It likely returned to the shore to rest and lay its eggs. Like all *Nothosaurs*, the front teeth were bigger than those at the back. The nostrils were at the top end of the snout so it could inhale (breathe in) air quickly when it came to the surface.

PREHISTORIC ANIMAL

TRIASSIC

This seal-like creature was part of one of the strongest groups of its time. It survived for more than 30 million years before being replaced by newer and faster marine reptiles.

PADDLES
Paddle-like limbs with five webbed fingers and toes made it a good swimmer, but its leg design shows that *Nothosaurus* was probably also comfortable on land.

WHERE IN THE WORLD?

Good fossils have been found in Germany, Italy, Netherlands, Switzerland, North Africa, China, Israel, and Russia.

HOW BIG IS IT?

TEETH
The broad, flat skull held dozens of sharp, interlocking teeth that helped it to hold on to its prey.

TIMELINE (millions of years ago)

540	505	438	408	360	280	248	208	146	65	1.8 to today

Shonisaurus

• ORDER • Ichthyosauria • FAMILY • Shastasauridae • GENUS & SPECIES • *Shonisaurus popularis & S. sikanniensis*

VITAL STATISTICS

FOSSIL LOCATION	North America
DIET	Carnivorous
PRONUNCIATION	SHO-ni-SAW-rus
WEIGHT	Unknown
LENGTH	as much as 70 ft (21 m)
HEIGHT	Unknown
MEANING OF NAME	"Shoshone Mountain lizard" because it was first discovered there

WHERE IN THE WORLD?

Shonisaurus has been found in Nevada and British Columbia, Canada. Another ichthyosaur found in the Himalayan Mountains, called *Himalayasaurus*, may be the same animal as *Shonisaurus*.

By far the largest marine reptile ever known, *Shonisaurus* was probably bigger and longer than today's sperm whale.

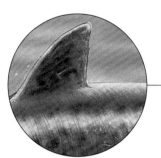

VERTEBRAE
When *Shonisaurus* vertebrae (parts of the spine) were first found in Nevada in the late 1800s, the miners working at the site used the huge disks like plates. They were big enough to hold meals!

FOSSIL EVIDENCE

Shonisaurus fossils were first discovered in the Triassic Luning Formation in Nevada. Dozens of *Shonisaurus popularis* skeletons were found together. This was the largest species of ichthyosaur at the time at 50 ft (15 m) long. *Shonisaurus sikanniensis* fossils, at up to 70 ft (21 m) long, were first found in the Triassic Pardonet Formation of British Columbia in 1991. Mosquitoes, bears, floods, and tough ground led to a dig that took years to complete. A helicopter was needed to airlift the 2-ton (1.8 tonne) blocks of stone out of the site before the fossil could be cleaned, described, and recorded.

TEETH
The young had tiny teeth in their jaws but probably lost them as they got older and began to eat different things.

PREHISTORIC ANIMAL

TRIASSIC

HOW BIG IS IT?

TIMELINE (millions of years ago)

540	505	438	408	360	280	248	208	146	65	1.8 to today

Dimorphodon

• **ORDER** • Pterosauria • **FAMILY** • Dimorphodontidae • **GENUS & SPECIES** • *Dimorphodon macronyx*

VITAL STATISTICS

FOSSIL LOCATION	England
DIET	Carnivorous
PRONUNCIATION	die-MORE-foe-don
WEIGHT	Unknown
LENGTH	3 ft (1 m) with 4 ft 6 in (1.4 m) wingspan
HEIGHT	Unknown
MEANING OF NAME	"Two-form tooth" because of its two types of teeth

FOSSIL EVIDENCE

Dimorphodon's flexible neck had to be strong to support its huge head. The large skull had cavities (holes) in the bone that cut down the weight of the thick head. *Dimorphodon* had a small brain. Although it was not one of the more intelligent prehistoric creatures, it survived by acting like a simple hunting machine. Always looking for fish, squid, or small reptiles, *Dimorphodon* would wait, watch, then swoop down to catch its meal.

PREHISTORIC ANIMAL

MID JURASSIC

A pterosaur from the early Jurassic, *Dimorphodon* swooped through the skies 180 million years ago. A flying reptile rather than a dinosaur, *Dimorphodon* was a dangerous predator with a huge head and large wingspan.

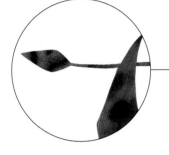

TAIL
A diamond-shaped flap of skin that was likely at the end of *Dimorphodon*'s tail helped the pterosaur stay balanced when it flew.

WHERE IN THE WORLD?

Lyme Regis, England, where *Dimorphodon* was found, is the home of Dinosaurland Fossil Museum.

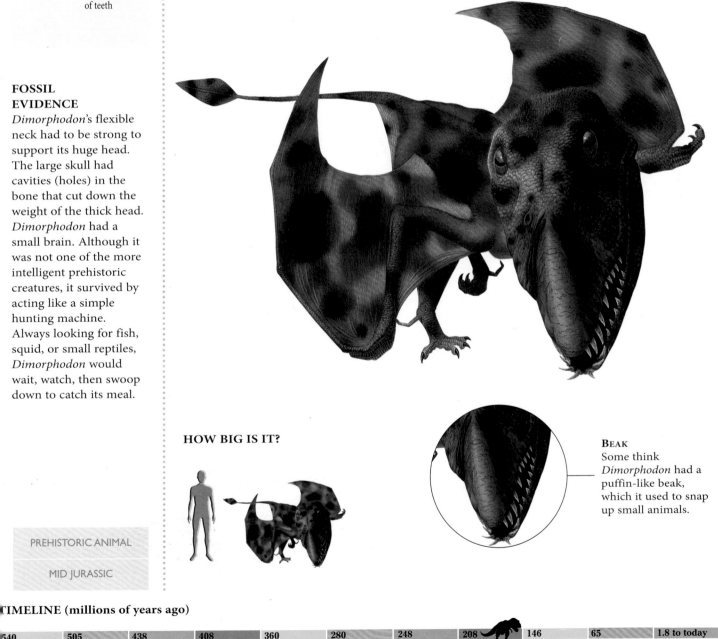

HOW BIG IS IT?

BEAK
Some think *Dimorphodon* had a puffin-like beak, which it used to snap up small animals.

TIMELINE (millions of years ago)

540	505	438	408	360	280	248	208	146	65	1.8 to today

Liopleurodon

• ORDER • Plesiosauria • FAMILY • Pliosauridae • GENUS & SPECIES • *Liopleurodon fero.*

VITAL STATISTICS

FOSSIL LOCATION	Europe
DIET	Carnivorous
PRONUNCIATION	LIE-oh-PLOOR-oh-don
WEIGHT	Unknown
LENGTH	23-33 ft (7-10 m)
HEIGHT	Unknown
MEANING OF NAME	"Smooth-sided tooth" because its teeth were smooth on one side

This plesiosaur was the top killer of Europe's Jurassic seas. A hunting, swimming reptile that lived at the same time as dinosaurs, *Liopleurodon* was one of the biggest plesiosaurs that ever lived.

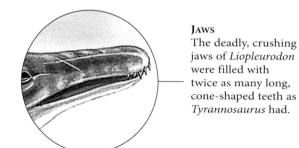

JAWS
The deadly, crushing jaws of *Liopleurodon* were filled with twice as many long, cone-shaped teeth as *Tyrannosaurus* had.

WHERE IN THE WORLD?

Liopleurodon swam in the depths of Europe's Late Jurassic seas, attacking prey from below.

FOSSIL EVIDENCE

Liopleurodon was in the top position on the marine food chain. This plesiosaur was fierce, probably hunting the seas for fish, smaller plesiosaurs, ichthyosaurs, and sharks. Its long skull measured 5 ft (1.5 m) long and supported muscles that powered a bite which might have been strong enough to crush the bones of any animal. *Liopleurodon* may have swam with its jaws open, letting water enter the nostril openings in the roof of its mouth. When water flowed out of the nasal openings near its eyes, *Liopleurodon* could smell the scent of its prey in the water.

PREHISTORIC ANIMAL

MID- LATE JURASSIC

HOW BIG IS IT?

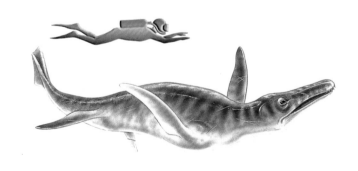

FLIPPERS
Four huge flippers moved *Liopleurodon* through the water, giving it the power to speed up quickly as it surprised its next meal.

TIMELINE (millions of years ago)

540	505	438	408	360	280	248	208	146	65	1.8 to today

Archaeopteryx

ORDER • Archaeopterygiformes • **FAMILY** • Archaeopterygidae
• **GENUS & SPECIES** • *Archaeopteryx lithographica*

VITAL STATISTICS

FOSSIL LOCATION	Germany
DIET	Carnivorous
PRONUNCIATION	Ark-ee-OP-ter-icks
WEIGHT	11-18 oz (300-500 g)
LENGTH	26 in (65 cm)
HEIGHT	12 in (30 cm)
MEANING OF NAME	"Ancient wing" because it is the oldest-known feathered animal

WHERE IN THE WORLD?

The limestone of southern Germany preserved (saved) the impressions of *Archaeopteryx*'s feathers.

Archaeopteryx is the earliest-known feathered animal. It has some features like today's birds and some features like non-avian theropods (theropods not related to birds). Some think this feathered animal is a missing link between the two.

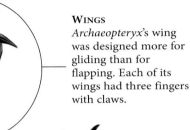

WINGS
Archaeopteryx's wing was designed more for gliding than for flapping. Each of its wings had three fingers with claws.

FOSSIL EVIDENCE

Archaeopteryx shows features of both birds and non-avian theropod dinosaurs. Its birdlike features include wings and feathers. Like non-avian theropods, it has a wishbone, hollow bones, toothed jaws, a long bony tail, and clawed hands. *Archaeopteryx* may have used its claws to climb the trunks of trees. Scientists disagree about how *Archaeopteryx* took flight. Some think it dropped out of trees. Others think it ran so fast (chasing small animals to eat) that it got airborne.

FEATHERS
Archaeopteryx's feathers warmed the early bird and controlled its body temperature. Like the feathers of modern birds, they also helped in flight.

HOW BIG IS IT?

DINOSAUR

LATE JURASSIC

TIMELINE (millions of years ago)

540	505	438	408	360	280	248	208	146	65	1.8 to today

Archaeopteryx

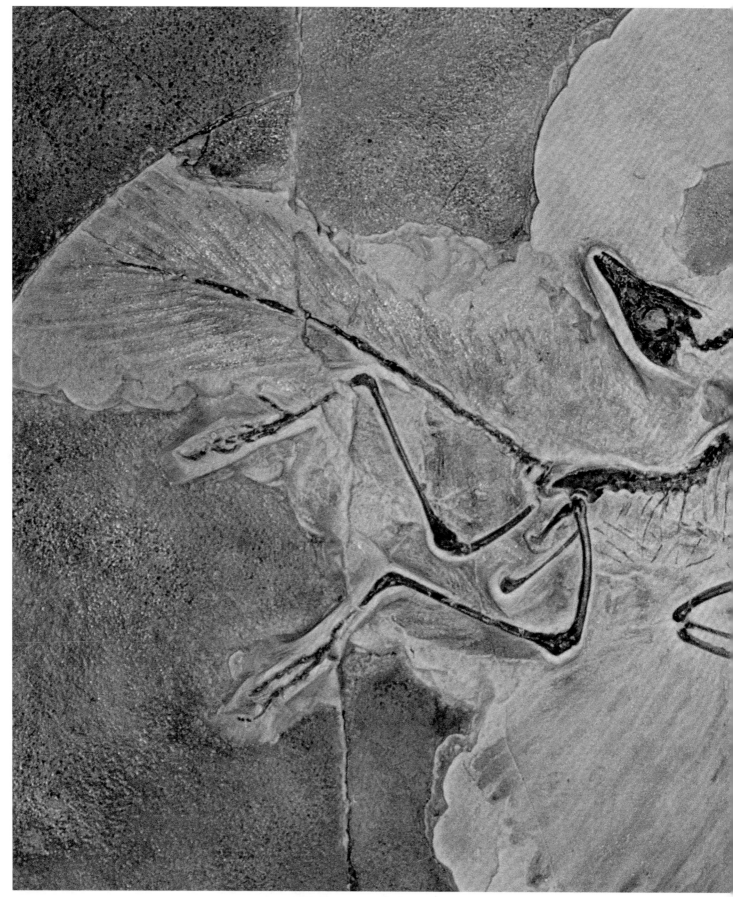

ORDER • Archaeopterygiformes • **FAMILY** • Archaeopterygidae • **GENUS & SPECIES** • *Archaeopteryx lithographica*

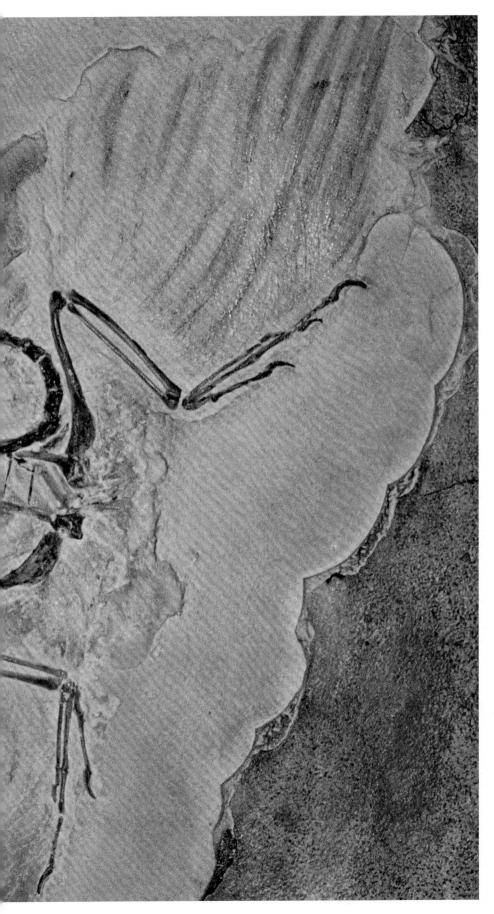

OLDEST-KNOWN BIRD

Many scientists argue about *Archaeopteryx*—the feathered animal from the Jurassic. Was it a bird? Was it a dinosaur? Or maybe neither? Could it fly? Was it a fake? There are eleven fossils, which give lots of clues. But there are still lots of questions about the connection between dinosaurs and birds. Even with the questions, though, many agree that the *Archaeopteryx* fossils are in fact from the oldest known bird.

Ophthalmosaurus

• **ORDER** • Ichthyosauria • **FAMILY** • Ophthalmosauridae • **GENUS & SPECIES** • *Ophthalmosaurus discus*

VITAL STATISTICS

FOSSIL LOCATION	Europe, North America, Argentina
DIET	Fish, mollusks, squid
PRONUNCIATION	Off-THAL-moh-SAWR-us
WEIGHT	3 tons (2.7 tonnes)
LENGTH	Up to 20 ft (6 m)
HEIGHT	Unknown
MEANING OF NAME	"Eye lizard" after its huge eyes

FOSSIL EVIDENCE

Ophthalmosaurus's most unique features were its oversized eyes. The larger the eye, the better the ichthyosaur was probably able to see in the murky depths of the ocean. *Ophthalmosaurus's* eyes had bony rings. These rings may have kept the eyes from changing shape, even under great water pressure. Even without too many teeth, *Ophthalmosaurus's* mighty jaws quickly snapped shut on smaller ocean creatures.

PREHISTORIC ANIMAL

LATE JURASSIC

Ophthalmosaurus was not a dinosaur, but an ichthyosaur, a prehistoric swimming reptile. Its huge, dolphin-shaped body cut through the warm Jurassic seas probably in search of fish and mollusks.

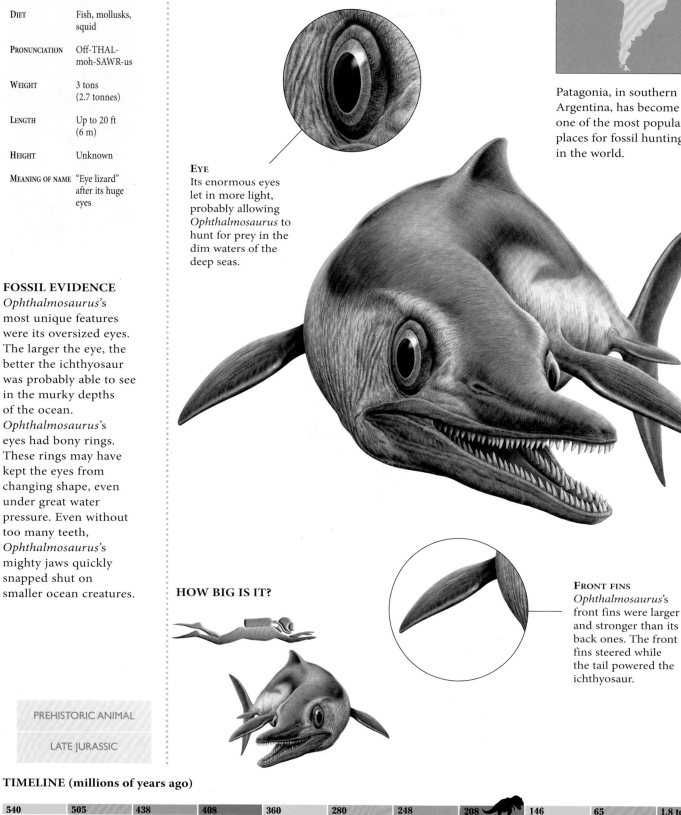

EYE
Its enormous eyes let in more light, probably allowing *Ophthalmosaurus* to hunt for prey in the dim waters of the deep seas.

HOW BIG IS IT?

FRONT FINS
Ophthalmosaurus's front fins were larger and stronger than its back ones. The front fins steered while the tail powered the ichthyosaur.

WHERE IN THE WORLD?

Patagonia, in southern Argentina, has become one of the most popular places for fossil hunting in the world.

TIMELINE (millions of years ago)

540	505	438	408	360	280	248	208	146	65	1.8 to today

Dsungaripterus

• **ORDER** • Pterosauria • **FAMILY** • Dsungaripteridae • **GENUS & SPECIES** • *Dsungaripterus weii*

VITAL STATISTICS

FOSSIL LOCATION	China
DIET	Crabs, fish, mollusks, plankton, insects
PRONUNCIATION	ZUNG-ah-RIP-tare-us
WEIGHT	22 lb (10 kg)
LENGTH	10 ft (3 m) wingspan
HEIGHT	Unknown
MEANING OF NAME	"Junggar wing" in honor of China's Junggar Basin where its fossil was found

FOSSIL EVIDENCE

Dsungaripterus's pointed, narrow jaws were toothless in front. It had blunt, toothlike knobs in the back of its jaw, which it probably used to crush shellfish. It lived along beaches where it may have picked small marine animals from between rocks with its narrow jaws. Scientists aren't sure how it used the strange crest on its snout. Discovery of a large number of *Dsungaripterus* fossils together is a clue that these pterosaurs may have lived in colonies (or groups) where they cared for their young.

PREHISTORIC ANIMAL

EARLY CRETACEOUS

Dsungaripterus was an Early Cretaceous pterosaur with a bony crest running along its snout. Its long, narrow jaws curved up toward the tip, giving them a tweezerlike appearance.

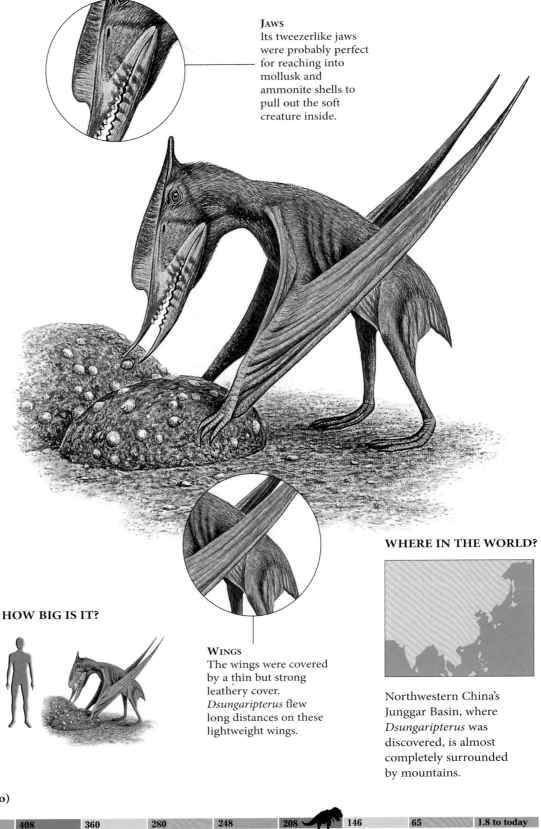

JAWS
Its tweezerlike jaws were probably perfect for reaching into mollusk and ammonite shells to pull out the soft creature inside.

HOW BIG IS IT?

WINGS
The wings were covered by a thin but strong leathery cover. *Dsungaripterus* flew long distances on these lightweight wings.

WHERE IN THE WORLD?

Northwestern China's Junggar Basin, where *Dsungaripterus* was discovered, is almost completely surrounded by mountains.

TIMELINE (millions of years ago)

540	505	438	408	360	280	248	208	146	65	1.8 to today

Tapejara

• **ORDER** • Pterosauria • **FAMILY** • Tapejaridae • **GENUS & SPECIES** • *Tapejara wellnhofer*

VITAL STATISTICS

FOSSIL LOCATION	Brazil
DIET	Unknown
PRONUNCIATION	Tah-pay-ZHAHR-a
WEIGHT	Up to 55 lb (25 kg)
LENGTH	5 ft (1.5 m) wingspan
HEIGHT	Unknown
MEANING OF NAME	"Old being" from the mythology of the Tupi Indians, who lived in the area where it was discovered

WHERE IN THE WORLD?

Tapejara was found in Brazil, near coastal areas.

Tapejara was a pterosaur rather than a dinosaur. It was part of the first group of vertebrates able to fly. It was small, with a skull only 8 in (20 cm) long, and had a short tail.

CREST
Its head crest was possibly brightly colored. It may have been used for display purposes.

FOSSIL EVIDENCE

Like all pterosaurs, *Tapejara* had extremely light bones. This means that its bones were likely to be crushed after death, so it was lucky that the first specimen was found in good shape. *Tapejara*'s strange skull was a surprise when first discovered. Scientists aren't exactly sure what it ate because they haven't found fossils of digested food (as they have for some other creatures). Since its discovery, several close relatives with similar skulls have been found. Its head crest may have worked like a rudder.

PREHISTORIC ANIMAL

EARLY CRETACEOUS

BEAK
Although *Tapejara* probably used its beak to eat fruit and berries, some paleontologists think it may have used its beak to catch fish.

HOW BIG IS IT?

TIMELINE (millions of years ago)

540	505	438	408	360	280	248	208	146	65	1.8 to today

Tropeognathus

• **ORDER** • Pterosauria • **FAMILY** • Criorhynchidae • **GENUS & SPECIES** • *Tropeognathus mesembrinus*

VITAL STATISTICS

FOSSIL LOCATION	Brazil
DIET	Probably fish and cephalopods
PRONUNCIATION	TROP-ee-og-NATH-us
WEIGHT	30 lb (14 kg)
LENGTH	20 ft (6.2 m) wingspan
HEIGHT	Unknown
MEANING OF NAME	"Keel jaw" because its jaw crest looked like a ship's keel

FOSSIL EVIDENCE

Many well-preserved fossils have been found in the Santana Formation in northeastern Brazil. The formation was found in 1828. Scientists continue to study the fossils found there and learn new things about the discoveries. *Tropeognathus* was first identified in 1987, from remains that, unfortunately, were not in very good shape. Because the fossil remains are unclear, scientists disagree about where to place this creature. Should this keel-jawed pterosaur be given its own genus (*Tropeognathus*) or should it be given the *Ornithocheirus* label?

PREHISTORIC ANIMAL

EARLY CRETACEOUS

Tropeognathus is known for the crests on its upper and lower jaws. They may have helped it keep a straight course as it skimmed through the water, fishing for prey.

BEAK
Possibly swooping to catch fish while in flight, *Tropeognathus* had a beak lined with sharp teeth designed for spearing fish.

WINGS
Tropeognathus used its large wings mostly for soaring and gliding.

WHERE IN THE WORLD?

Tropeognathus was found in Brazil.

HOW BIG IS IT?

TIMELINE (millions of years ago)

540	505	438	408	360	280	248	208	146	65	1.8 to today

Kronosaurus

• **ORDER** • Plesiosauria • **FAMILY** • Pliosauridae • **GENUS & SPECIES** • *Kronosaurus queenslandicu.*

VITAL STATISTICS

FOSSIL LOCATION	Australia, Colombia
DIET	Carnivorous
PRONUNCIATION	KRON-oh-SAWR-us
WEIGHT	Up to 22 tons (24 tonnes)
LENGTH	23-30 ft (7-9 m)
HEIGHT	Unknown
MEANING OF NAME	"Titan lizard," after the Titan Kronos of Greek mythology, because of its large size and appetite

FOSSIL EVIDENCE

Kronosaurus is known from several specimens, one with a skull 9 ft (3 m) long (about one-third of its whole body length). Many of the specimens are in bad shape. The most famous fossil is part of a skeleton which is kept at Harvard University in Massachusetts. But dynamite was used to get the fossil out, and that might have destroyed some clues. When it was rebuilt, large amounts of plaster of paris were used, which helped give it its nickname Plasterosaurus. Today the reconstruction (model built from fossil evidence) is thought to be about 13 ft (4 m) too long.

PREHISTORIC ANIMAL

EARLY CRETACEOUS

Kronosaurus was a reptile that lived in the open seas, breathing air. It probably fed on fish, mollusks, and other reptiles, including sharks. It is unknown whether it laid its eggs on land or had live births at sea.

FLIPPERS
Four paddle-like flippers moved *Kronosaurus* through the water at great speed, and may have helped it to move on land like modern seals.

MOUTH
With muscle-packed jaws and front teeth up to 9 in (23 cm) long, *Kronosaurus* was a fierce predator.

WHERE IN THE WORLD?

Kronosaurus swam the shallow inland seas that covered Australia and Colombia.

HOW BIG IS IT?

TIMELINE (millions of years ago)

540	505	438	408	360	280	248	208	146	65	1.8 to today

Pterodaustro

• **ORDER** • Pterosauria • **FAMILY** • Ctenochasmatidae • **GENUS & SPECIES** • *Pterodaustro guinazui*

VITAL STATISTICS

FOSSIL LOCATION	Argentina
DIET	Possibly omnivorous
PRONUNCIATION	ter-ah-DAWS-tro
WEIGHT	Unknown
LENGTH	52 in (132 cm)
HEIGHT	Unknown
MEANING OF NAME	"Wing from the South"

One of the strangest pterosaurs, *Pterodaustro* had a mouth full of long, thin, flexible teeth that were probably used as a strainer or filter.

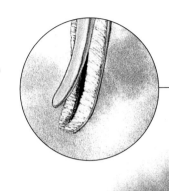

TEETH
Pterodaustro's amazing lower teeth were paired with tiny, globe-shaped teeth in the upper jaws, which may have been used to mash its food.

WHERE IN THE WORLD?

This strange pterosaur is known only from San Luis Province in Argentina.

FOSSIL EVIDENCE

This pterosaur's fossils were first found in 1970. The rocks where they were found seem to have come from the bottoms of lakes. Scientists also found complete fossils of an early fish (called a semionotid) in the same area. The fossils from this area are often colored bluish-green. They change color after they dry out. The fossils are delicate. A special "paint" is used to keep them from breaking easily.

EGGS
One of the three known pterosaur eggs is from *Pterodaustro*. It shows the embryo curled up inside shortly before it would have hatched.

HOW BIG IS IT?

PREHISTORIC ANIMAL

EARLY CRETACEOUS

DID YOU KNOW?
Because of the likely filter-feeding habit of this animal, it is often called the flamingo pterosaur. Some artists have even colored *Pterodaustro* pink when making models of the creature.

TIMELINE (millions of years ago)

40	505	438	408	360	280	248	208	146	65	1.8 to today

Elasmosaurus

• **ORDER** • Plesiosauria • **FAMILY** • Elasmosaurida
• **GENUS & SPECIES** • Several species within the genus *Elasmosauru*

VITAL STATISTICS

FOSSIL LOCATION	Asia, North America
DIET	Carnivorous
PRONUNCIATION	Eh-LAZZ-mo-SAWR-us
WEIGHT	4 tons (4.4 tonnes)
LENGTH	46 ft (14 m)
HEIGHT	Unknown
MEANING OF NAME	"Plate lizard" because of its plate-like shoulder bones

FOSSIL EVIDENCE

Elasmosaurus was first rebuilt from fossils in 1868 by the paleontologist Edward Cope, who made a mistake and thought the long neck was the tail. Because *Elasmosaurus*'s neck is so heavy, it could probably only lift its head above the water. It also had four stiff flippers. These clues make scientists think that *Elasmosaurus* probably lived in the open seas and did not come on land. It probably moved slowly even in the water.

PREHISTORIC ANIMAL

LATE CRETACEOUS

The long-necked *Elasmosaurus* had up to 75 vertebrae. (This is a huge number when you think that most of today's mammals have between seven and eight.) It lived in the open water and breathed air like today's dolphins.

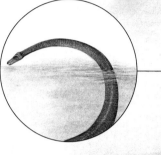

NECK
At 26 ft (8 m) long, its neck was half the total length of *Elasmosaurus*, helping it to surprise and catch prey.

HEAD
Its small head cut down what it could swallow, and *Elasmosaurus* probably survived on small fish, squid, and ammonites.

HOW BIG IS IT?

WHERE IN THE WORLD?

Elasmosaurus was found in Japan and in the inland sea covering the western part of North America.

TIMELINE (millions of years ago)

540	505	438	408	360	280	248	208	146	65	1.8 to today

Xiphactinus

• **ORDER** • Pachycormiformes • **FAMILY** • Ichthyodectidae • **GENUS & SPECIES** • *Xiphactinus audax*

VITAL STATISTICS

FOSSIL LOCATION	North America
DIET	Carnivorous
PRONUNCIATION	Zy-FACT-in-us
WEIGHT	500 lb (227 kg)
LENGTH	14-17 ft (4.3-5.1 m)
HEIGHT	Unknown
MEANING OF NAME	"Sword ray" for the swordlike fin rays of its pectoral fins

FOSSIL EVIDENCE

Many *Xiphactinus* have been found with the remains of prey in their stomachs. It is thought that this happened when prey struggled after being swallowed whole. The struggle would have torn the *Xiphactinus*'s stomach, causing it to die. A *Xiphactinus* fossil with a *Gillicus* in its gut is displayed at the Sternberg Museum of Natural History in Kansas. In 2002, an incomplete skull was found in the Czech Republic and may be a new species of *Xiphactinus*.

PREHISTORIC ANIMAL

LATE CRETACEOUS

An efficient predator, *Xiphactinus* could swim at very high speeds. It may have stunned prey with a smack of its forked tail. It may have leaped above the waves to remove parasites from its body.

MOUTH
Xiphactinus's upturned jaw could open wide enough to let this fish swallow prey the size of a human adult whole.

WHERE IN THE WORLD?

Xiphactinus swam in the Western Interior Seaway, above what is now the middle of North America.

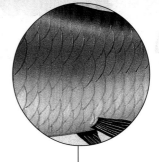

BODY
A dark bluish black and silver belly meant that *Xiphactinus* may have been dark above and light below. This is a common type of camouflage for ocean fish.

HOW BIG IS IT?

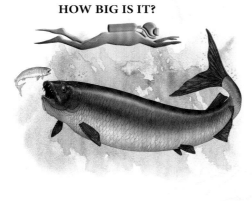

TIMELINE (millions of years ago)

40	505	438	408	360	280	248	208	146	65	1.8 to today

Xiphactinus

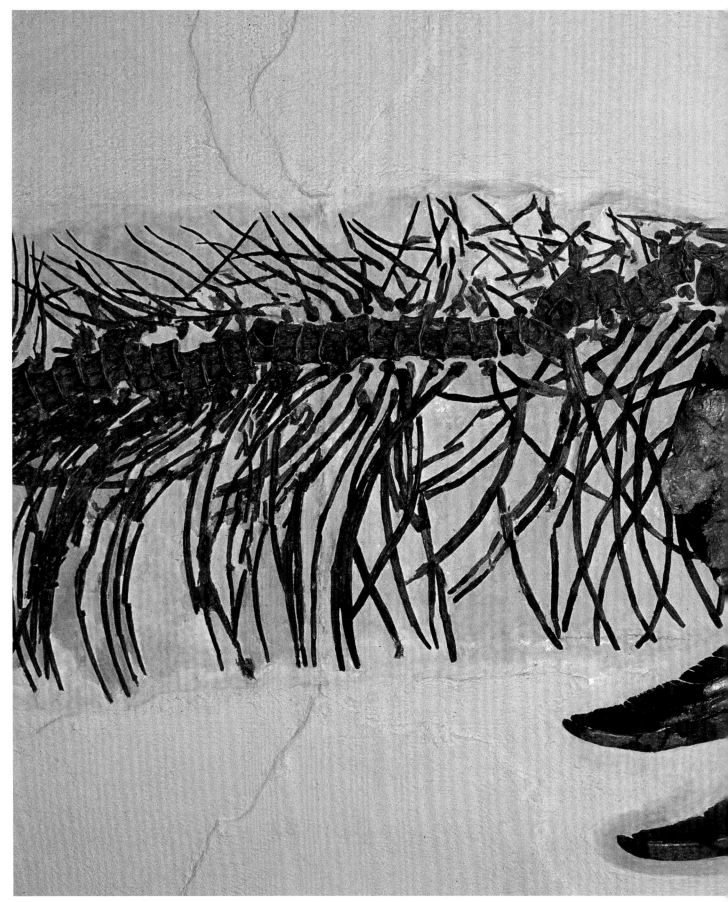

• ORDER • Pachycormiformes **• FAMILY •** Ichthyodectidae **• GENUS & SPECIES •** *Xiphactinus audax*

TIGER-FANGED SEA PREDATOR

Xiphactinus looked like a giant cousin of the modern fish known as the tarpon. *Xiphactinus* belonged to the long extinct order Ichthyodectiformes. In 1872, it was described as having a "head as long or longer than that of a fully grown grizzly bear," a snout "shorter and deeper than that of a bulldog," and teeth "being thus as long as the fangs of a tiger, but more slender," which were part of a powerful set of jaws. Since then, huge fossils of *Xiphactinus* have been common finds in the sediments left behind from North America's Western Interior Seaway. This shallow sea divided the continent in the Late Cretaceous and left deposits of chalk in which the fossils of ancient sharks, bony fish, turtles, mosasaurs, plesiosaurs, dinosaurs, and pterosaurs have been found. The Western Interior Seaway's sediment was made of a fine chalk and it built up without being washed away. Because of this, many complete fossils have been found here, including a *Xiphactinus* with its last meal in its guts.

Tylosaurus

• ORDER • Squamata • FAMILY • Mosasauridae • GENUS & SPECIES • Various species within the genus *Tylosauru*

VITAL STATISTICS

FOSSIL LOCATION	United States, New Zealand
DIET	Carnivorous
PRONUNCIATION	TY-lo-SORE-us
WEIGHT	11 tons (10 tonnes)
LENGTH	49 ft (15 m)
HEIGHT	Unknown
MEANING OF NAME	"Knob lizard" because its snout extended well beyond the foremost teeth

FOSSIL EVIDENCE

Complete *Tylosaurus* fossils are common. The first specimen was found near Monument Rocks, Kansas, in 1868. The rocks in this area are called the Niobrara Chalk. They are famous for their abundant fossils of mosasaurs and other marine reptiles, fish, bivalves, and other Late Cretaceous marine organisms. Even giant squid have been found here and may have been prey for *Tylosaurus*. The fine-grained nature of the chalk sediments ensured the detailed preservation of the fossils found there.

PREHISTORIC ANIMAL

LATE CRETACEOUS

WHERE IN THE WORLD?

Fossils of *Tylosaurus* are very common in the United States. Tylosaurs are also known from New Zealand.

Tylosaurus was one of the top marine predators of its time and the largest mosasaur in its environment.

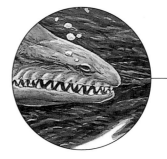

SNOUT
The projecting snout of *Tylosaurus* may have been used to ram into prey or in combat with others of its kind, but it was probably too sensitive for this purpose.

HOW BIG IS IT?

TEETH
Tylosaurus's teeth were replaced, as needed, throughout the life of the animal.

TIMELINE (millions of years ago)

540	505	438	408	360	280	248	208	146	65	1.8 to today

Quetzalcoatlus

• **ORDER** • Pterosauria • **FAMILY** • Azhdarchidae • **GENUS & SPECIES** • *Quetzalcoatlus northropi*

VITAL STATISTICS

FOSSIL LOCATION	North America
DIET	Carnivorous
PRONUNCIATION	Kett-zal-coe-AT-luss
WEIGHT	220 lb (100 kg)
WINGSPAN	36 ft (11 m)
HEIGHT	22 ft (7 m)
MEANING OF NAME	"Plumed serpent" from the name of the Aztec and Toltec feathered snake god

FOSSIL EVIDENCE

Quetzalcoatlus probably walked on all fours but was best suited to flight. Its enormous wings allowed it to glide on warm air currents and breezes. Its paper-thin, hollow bones supported a light, streamlined body with a long neck holding a head topped by a bony crest. It lived inland and probably fished over lakes and rivers. It may also have been a scavenger, meaning it ate the flesh from the bodies of dead animals.

PREHISTORIC ANIMAL

LATE CRETACEOUS

This was one of the largest flying animals the world has seen. A pterosaur rather than a dinosaur, it glided on large wings that may have measured 36 ft (11 m) from tip to tip.

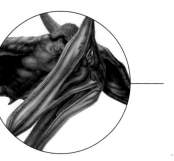

NECK
The neck is estimated at 8 ft (2.4 m) long. It was held upright by tendons and muscles, which allowed *Quetzalcoatlus* to stay streamlined in flight.

WHERE IN THE WORLD?

Quetzalcoatlus was first discovered in Big Bend National Park, Texas, and later in Alberta, Canada.

WINGS
The wings were covered by a thin, leathery skin stretched between its body, the tops of its legs, and its long fourth fingers.

HOW BIG IS IT?

TIMELINE (millions of years ago)

540	505	438	408	360	280	248	208	146	65	1.8 to today

Quetzalcoatlus

• **ORDER** • Pterosauria • **FAMILY** • Azhdarchidae • **GENUS & SPECIES** • *Quetzalcoatlus northropi*

CHANGING WINGSPAN IDEAS

Before the first *Quetzalcoatlus* fossils were found in the early 1970s, some researchers had different ideas about the maximum possible size of flying animals. Using models, they reasoned that the *Pteranodon* was at the absolute upper size limit for a flying animal. In fact, the *Pteranodon* was considered the record-holder for the all-time largest vertebrate flier for many years. The lesson here is that models can be flawed and that the final answers need to come from actual fossils. But another lesson to learn from *Quetzalcoatlus* is that size estimates made using partial fossils must be taken with a grain of salt. The first approximation of the wingspan based on partial *Quetzalcoatlus* fossils was 50 ft (15.3 m). Now, 33-40 ft (10-12.2 m) is a much more trusted estimate. Clearly, ideas in paleontology change as new fossils are found.

Libonectes

• **ORDER** • Plesiosauria • **FAMILY** • Elasmosauridae • **GENUS & SPECIES** • *Libonectes morgani* and *L. atlasense*

VITAL STATISTICS

FOSSIL LOCATION	United States
DIET	Carnivorous
PRONUNCIATION	lee-bon-EK-teez
WEIGHT	5.5-9 tons (5-8 tonnes)
LENGTH	23-26 ft (7-14 m)
HEIGHT	Unknown
MEANING OF NAME	"Southwest swimmer" because it was found in the Southwest

FOSSIL EVIDENCE

One early fossil hunter thought the neck of *Libonectes*'s relatives was a tail, because they had never seen a creature shaped like it. At the time, it was believed that their necks were as flexible as a snake's body. Now it is known that the neck was pretty inflexible. *Libonectes* is thought to have used its swimming skills to follow schools of fish and attack from underneath, trapping them in its cage-like mouth. It swallowed rocks, which may have been used to improve its balance in the water.

PREHISTORIC ANIMAL

LATE CRETACEOUS

Libonectes **was a type of very long-necked plesiosaur known as an elasmosaur, a group of marine animals with four strong, paddlelike flippers that swam in the Late Cretaceous seas.**

NECK
There were 62 bones in the long neck, which made up almost half of the length of *Libonectes*'s body.

WHERE IN THE WORLD?

Remains have been found in Texas and Kansas.

TEETH
There were up to 36 long, sharp, forward-facing teeth. These interlinked to form a cage for trapping fish and squid.

HOW BIG IS IT?

TIMELINE (millions of years ago)

540	505	438	408	360	280	248	208	146	65	1.8 to today

Mosasaur

• ORDER • Squamata **• FAMILY •** Mosasauridae **• GENUS & SPECIES •** Various

VITAL STATISTICS

FOSSIL LOCATION	Worldwide
DIET	Carnivorous
PRONUNCIATION	MO-za-sore
WEIGHT	At least 20 tons (18 tonnes) for the largest ones
LENGTH	57 ft (17 m)
HEIGHT	Unknown
MEANING OF NAME	"Meuse lizard" because the first one named was discovered near the Meuse River in the Netherlands

Mosasaurs were a type of large marine squamate. Squamates are a group of animals made up of lizards and snakes, and mosasaurs included the largest squamates of all time. Mosasaurs were large marine animals that evolved paddle-like limbs and flattened tails for swimming after their land-dwelling ancestors entered the sea.

WHERE IN THE WORLD?

Mosasaur fossils have been found on every continent in marine sediments of the Late Cretaceous. They are especially well known from the Western Interior Seaway deposits of North America.

FORELIMBS
These flippers were useful for moving around in the water. Their finger bones, which were inside the flippers, were more numerous than in the human hand.

FOSSIL EVIDENCE

Although teeth and bone fragments can be found in most places where mosasaurs lived, they are well known from the numerous complete skeletons that have been found. Mosasaurs have a very good fossil record because dead marine animals have a better chance of being buried and preserved than do land animals. Mosasaurs were very common worldwide in the Late Cretaceous Period. They became extinct at the end of the Cretaceous Period, along with all of the non-avian dinosaurs and certain other groups.

TEETH
Mosasaurs were all flesh eaters. Most had mouths full of sharp teeth, which were replaced throughout their lives.

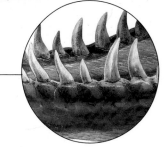

HOW BIG IS IT?

PREHISTORIC ANIMAL

LATE CRETACEOUS

TIMELINE (millions of years ago)

540	505	438	408	360	280	248	208	146	65	1.8 to today

Mosasaur

• **ORDER** • Squamata • **FAMILY** • Mosasauridae • **GENUS & SPECIES** • Various

FOSSIL TREASURE

The best-known mosasaur fossil has a bizarre history. Now on display at the Teylers Museum in Haarlem, it was found in a chalk quarry in the Netherlands in the early 1770s. It was first identified as a crocodile, and later, in 1786, as a sperm whale. In 1794, the by-then-famous fossil was taken as a war treasure by a geologist who was with the occupying French armies led by Napoleon Bonaparte. After it was noticed that the fossil was removed from the cottage in which its first owner had displayed it, an offer was made of "six hundred bottles of good wine" to the first troops able to locate the skull. The bargain worked and the fossil then became a specimen in the Muséum National d'Histoire Naturelle in Paris. It didn't get its general name *Mosasaurus* until 1822, and its species name *M. hoffmanni* until 1829. This photo shows another mosasaur fossil on display in Maastricht, Netherlands.

Pteranodon

VITAL STATISTICS

FOSSIL LOCATION	United States
DIET	Fish
PRONUNCIATION	Teh-RAH-noh-don
WEIGHT	35 lb (15.8 kg)
LENGTH	Up to 30 ft (9 m)
HEIGHT	6 ft (1.8 m)
MEANING OF NAME	"Winged and toothless"

FOSSIL EVIDENCE

Pteranodon fossils were collected at the Smoky Hill Chalk in the north of the Niobrara Formation in western Kansas as early as 1870. *Pteranodon sternbergi* is recognized as the likely ancestor of a later species of *Pteranodon*. *Pteranodon longiceps* was named in 1876 from an almost complete fossil that had a wingspan of 23 ft (7 m). Fossilized fish bones found in the specimen's stomach proved that these creatures ate fish.

PREHISTORIC ANIMAL

LATE CRETACEOUS

Pteranodon is one of the largest pterosaurs, or flying reptiles. They lived around 89.3 million years ago in what is now the central region of the United States. *Pteranodon*, one of the last pterosaurs, was once thought to be the largest creature that could fly. Except for its enormous size, *Pteranodon* looked like present-day birds because its beak had no teeth and its bones were hollow. Its huge wingspan is like that of a small aircraft, which made it a true giant of the air. *Pteranodon*'s long, pointed beak made it ideal for diving into the sea to catch the fish on which it lived.

HUGE FEMALE
It is thought that the female *Pteranodon* was two-thirds the size of the male. They were still huge, with a wingspan measuring 20 ft (6 m) across.

HOW BIG IS IT?

FEET
Pteranodon was not a dinosaur but a pterosaur, in part because it stood semi-upright, not totally upright as dinosaurs do.

• ORDER • Pterosauria **• FAMILY •** Pteranodontidae **• GENUS & SPECIES •** *Pteranodon longiceps, P. sternbergi*

NO TEETH

When the first wingbone fragments of *Pteranodon* were found in 1870, this Late Cretaceous flying reptile was confused with the *Pterodactylus*. In 1876, the first skulls were found and it was discovered that, unlike *Pterodactylus*, this creature had no teeth. That was when the fossils were renamed *Pteranodon*, meaning "no teeth."

CREST
The long crest may have balanced the heavy bill.

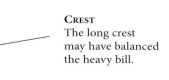

WHERE IN THE WORLD?

Pteranodon remains have been found in Kansas, Alabama, Nebraska, Wyoming, and South Dakota.

TOOTHLESS
Unlike the *Pterodactylus*, with which this flying reptile was once confused, *Pteranodon* had no teeth in its beak.

BIG-HEADED FLYING MONSTER

Pteranodon was well-equipped to fly. But, it probably spent more of its time soaring through the prehistoric skies than flapping its wings. *Pteranodon's* hollow bones cut down its body weight, and the vertebrae in its back were joined to its ribs to provide good support for the flying muscles. *Pteranodon* was still a rather odd-looking creature, because its head, with its long pointed beak, was larger than the trunk of its body.

TIMELINE (millions of years ago)

540	505	438	408	360	280	248	208	146	65	1.8 to today

33

Pteranodon

• **ORDER** • Pterosauria • **FAMILY** • Pteranodontidae • **GENUS & SPECIES** • *Pteranodon longiceps, P. sternbergi*

MYSTERIOUS CREST

Pteranodon had two features that really stood out. First, it had a very short tail, while earlier pterosaurs had long tails. Second, it carried a very long, bony crest that, in some of these flying reptiles, doubled the length of its head. Together, *Pteranodon*'s head and crest measured around 6 ft (1.8 m). No one is certain what the crest was for, although there have been several suggestions. One is that the crest balanced the long beak—important for *Pteranodon*'s balance in flight. Another is that the crest was used as a kind of rudder to help in landing. The crest might even have acted as a brake to stop the *Pteranodon* from landing too quickly and hurting itself. Some *Pteranodon* had no crest at all. Some scientists think that it may have been a characteristic of males, possibly used for display to attract females during mating. Whatever role the crest played, *Pteranodon*'s skill in the air may not have been all that great. Despite a wingspan of over 27 ft (8 m,) it may have done more gliding than flying.

Hesperornis

• **ORDER** • Hesperornithiformes • **FAMILY** • Hesperornithida
• **GENUS & SPECIES** • Several species within the genus *Hesperorn*

Hesperornis was a huge bird that could not fly or walk on land but was a fast swimmer and skilled diver. It was one of the greatest predators of the ocean.

VITAL STATISTICS

FOSSIL LOCATION	North America
DIET	Carnivorous
PRONUNCIATION	hess-puh-RAWR-nihs
WEIGHT	Unknown
LENGTH	5 ft (1.5 m)
HEIGHT	Unknown
MEANING OF NAME	"Western bird" because it was found in the western US

WHERE IN THE WORLD?

Hesperornis hunted in the Western Interior Seaway, the Turgai Strait, and the prehistoric North Sea.

FOSSIL EVIDENCE

This was one of the largest birds of the Age of Dinosaurs. On land, *Hesperornis* could only dig with its legs and push itself along on its belly like a sea turtle, making it very easy prey on land. It may have nested on isolated islands or stayed in the sea and given birth to live young. In water, it could dive and swim, powered by backward-facing legs with webbed feet.

BEAK
The beak featured many sharp teeth for gripping prey — a feature unknown in birds after the Mesozoic.

LEGS
The legs were not strong enough to support *Hesperornis*'s weight on land. The legs were turned backward, which would make them useful for swimming.

HOW BIG IS IT?

DINOSAUR
LATE CRETACEOUS

TIMELINE (millions of years ago)

540	505	438	408	360	280	248	208	146	65	1.8 to today

Mammalodon

• **ORDER** • Cetacea • **FAMILY** • Mammalodontidae • **GENUS & SPECIES** • *Mammalodon colliveri*

VITAL STATISTICS

FOSSIL LOCATION	Australia
DIET	Carnivorous
PRONUNCIATION	Mamm-AL-oh-don
WEIGHT	Unknown
LENGTH	8 ft (2.5 m)
HEIGHT	Unknown
MEANING OF NAME	"Mammal tooth" because its teeth apparently showed its mammalian heritage

FOSSIL EVIDENCE

Mammalodon, which was discovered in 1932, was an early type of baleen whale. Unlike present-day baleen whales, its mouth had teeth, but also may have featured baleen plates. These plates allow a whale to filter food from mouthfuls of water. Its face was short and its jaw contained only one or two incisor teeth, which are sharp cutting teeth. *Mammalodon*'s teeth were widely spaced, but it has not yet been determined whether or not it could filter small marine animals through its whalebones. *Janjucetus*, a longer-toothed specimen of the same period, was found on the same Australian beach (Jan Juc) in the late 1990s.

PREHISTORIC ANIMAL

TERTIARY (OLIGOCENE)

Mammalodon colliveri **was the first toothed baleen whale ever discovered. English paleontologist George Pritchard spotted one of its skull bones on Jan Juc Beach, in Torquay, Victoria, in Australia.**

BODY
Mammalodon was much smaller and more primitive than today's whales.

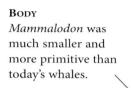

TEETH
Mammalodon was small compared to modern whales. It had teeth as well as baleen plates.

WHERE IN THE WORLD?

Mammalodon fossils were found in Torquay in the state of Victoria, Australia.

HOW BIG IS IT?

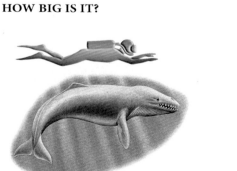

Basilosaurus

VITAL STATISTICS

FOSSIL LOCATION	US, Egypt, Pakistan
DIET	Carnivorous
PRONUNCIATION	Baz-illo-SAWR-us
WEIGHT	6.1 tons (6,300 kg)
LENGTH	150 ft (45 m)
HEIGHT	Unknown
MEANING OF NAME	"King lizard" because it was first thought to be a marine reptile

FOSSIL EVIDENCE

The great length of *Basilosaurus* was because of the length and number of its vertebrae. It was once described as "the nearest a whale ever came to a snake." *Basilosaurus* could move like an eel, but it moved up and down instead of side to side. Its vertebrae seem to have been hollow and were probably filled with fluid. Recently, fossils of *Basilosaurus*'s tiny hind legs were found but they clearly showed that they were not supposed to move around on land.

PREHISTORIC ANIMAL

TERTIARY (EOCENE)

Basilosaurus was a marine mammal that lived in the prehistoric ocean some 40 million years ago. Its bones were first discovered in the early nineteenth century in Alabama. But it was not too well known until 1845, when the paleontologist Albert Koch built a model of a giant 115-foot (35 m)-long skeleton and called it a sea serpent. Later, it turned out that the bones came from five different creatures and that the so-called sea serpent was a fake. After that, though, a very well-preserved species of *Basilosaurus* was found in the Wadi Al-Hitan (Arabic for "Whale Valley") in Egypt, and remains of another species were found in Pakistan.

BODY SHAPE
Despite its enormous size, the sleek, streamlined body of *Basilosaurus* slid through the water with grace and ease.

TEETH
The teeth were pointed at the front of the jaw and saw-edged at the rear.

• **ORDER** • Cetacea • **FAMILY** • Basilosauridae • **GENUS & SPECIES** • Several species within the genus *Basilosaurus*

PROOF OF LIMBS
Basilosaurus's 2-foot (60-cm) long hind limbs were clues that its earlier relatives may have walked on land. They weren't useful for moving through water. Earlier *Basilosaurus* had been land creatures and these tiny limbs were what was left of the legs that they used to walk on.

DID YOU KNOW?
Basilosaurus is the state fossil of both Mississippi and Alabama, where paleontologists first discovered its remains.

HOW BIG IS IT?

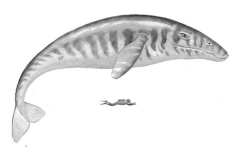

FOSSIL FURNITURE
In 1834, so many fossils of one *Basilosaurus* species, *B. cetoides*, were being found in Louisiana and Alabama that local people were turning them into pieces of furniture. Dr. Richard Harlan got some of these fossils and realized that material of great scientific value was being destroyed. Harlan named the fossils *Basilosaurus* and a fellow scientist, Sir Richard Owen, later suggested that they belonged to a mammal.

WHERE IN THE WORLD?

Remains have been found in Alabama, in Egypt's Zeuglodon Valley, and in Pakistan.

TIMELINE (millions of years ago)

| 540 | 505 | 438 | 408 | 360 | 280 | 248 | 208 | 146 | 65 | 1.8 to today |

Basilosaurus

• **ORDER** • Cetacea • **FAMILY** • Basilosauridae • **GENUS & SPECIES** • Several species within the genus *Basilosaurus*

FAKE SEA SERPENT

In the early days of paleontology, it was pretty easy to fool the public, and even other paleontologists, into believing that an exciting new prehistoric creature had been discovered. This is what happened in 1845 when Albert Koch learned that giant bones had been found in Alabama. Koch traveled there to see the remains. He decided to create an enormous skeleton and put it on display. Koch built a massive skeleton 115 ft (35 m) in length, which he described as a sea serpent that was longer, larger, and taller than any dinosaur known in the mid-nineteenth century. Today we know that such measurements would have made the fake sea serpent similar in size to the 115-foot (35 m)-long titanosaurian *Argentinosaurus*, which was first described in 1993. But, at the time, Koch's sea serpent became a great success when put on display in New York City and when it was shown across Europe. It was, of course, a fake—built with real fossils of several animals put together incorrectly. Later, it was discovered that the skeleton came from five creatures, not all of which were *Basilosaurus*. Koch's sea serpent ended up being lost in the Great Fire of Chicago in 1871.

Argentavis

VITAL STATISTICS

FOSSIL LOCATION	Argentina
DIET	Carnivorous
PRONUNCIATION	ar-jen-TAY-viss
WEIGHT	140-180 lb (63-80 kg)
LENGTH	26 ft (8 m)
HEIGHT	5 ft (1.5 m)
MEANING OF NAME	"Argentine bird"

FOSSIL EVIDENCE

Flying birds need very lightweight skeletons to in order to fly. Their bones are often hollow with thin, delicate walls. They can break easily. Because of this, bird fossils are uncommon. The bird fossils that are found are often broken into pieces. No complete skeletons exist of *Argentavis*, but a model has been made from the scattered bits available. *Argentavis* fossils have been found from the foothills of the Andes to the pampas (grass-covered plains). This gives scientists clues that the bird may have used the wind (from the mountains) and the warm air currents (from the plains) to help it take flight.

DINOSAUR

TERTIARY (MIOCENE)

The largest flying bird ever known, *Argentavis* **glided high above its territory looking for prey to surprise and attack.**

Argentavis comes from Argentina. So far, no fossils of this bird have been found anywhere else.

WINGS
Gliders need large wings to travel long distances without flapping. Scientists guess the area of *Argentavis*'s wings was 75 sq ft (7 sq m).

• **ORDER** • Ciconiiformes • **FAMILY** • Teratornithidae • **GENUS & SPECIES** • *Argentavis magnificens*

Argentavis was a huge Miocene flying bird. It had a wingspan that may have reached 26 ft (8 m) and it weighed over 140 lb (63 kg). The wandering albatross has the largest wingspan of today's birds, at 12 ft (3.6 m). And today's heaviest birds weigh about 40-45 lb (18-20 kg). Comparing these numbers gives you an idea of how enormous *Argentavis* was. Its humerus bone (long bone of the forelimb) alone was as long as an adult human arm.

BEAK
The hook at the end of *Argentavis*'s beak is common for a flesh-eating bird. But, other skull features give clues that it swallowed much of its food whole.

HOW BIG IS IT?

DID YOU KNOW?
Argentavis was probably too big to keep its wings flapping for a long time. It used the wind and rising heat (from the ground) to help get its huge body airborne.

TIMELINE (millions of years ago)

| 40 | 505 | 438 | 408 | 360 | 280 | 248 | 208 | 146 | 65 | 1.8 to today |

Carcharocles

• ORDER • Lamniformes • FAMILY • Lamnidae • GENUS & SPECIES • *Carcharocles megalodo*

VITAL STATISTICS

FOSSIL LOCATION	Worldwide
DIET	Carnivorous
PRONUNCIATION	car-CAR-o-kleez MEG-ah-lo-don
WEIGHT	50 tons (45,360 kg)
LENGTH	60 ft (18 m)
HEIGHT	Unknown
MEANING OF NAME	"Jagged clamp" or "Jagged and famous"

FOSSIL EVIDENCE

Giant teeth of prehistoric sharks have been around for hundreds of years. Shark teeth are probably the most common vertebrate fossils because sharks have a long, interesting history. There are (and were) lots of sharks around and they grow (and lose) thousands of strong teeth during their lifetimes. These teeth make great fossils. But little else of the skeletons of these animals is known. This is because sharks have skeletons made of cartilage that don't often preserve well. In some rare cases, jaws and vertebrae have been found. Along with the teeth, these give scientists clues that *Carcharocles megalodon* possibly grew to 60 ft (18 m) in length.

PREHISTORIC ANIMAL

NEOGENE

WHERE IN THE WORLD?

Teeth of *C. megalodon* (sometimes called just *Megalodon*) have been found worldwide. They have even been dug up from the South Pacific sea floor.

Imagine a prehistoric shark so huge that it preyed on whales; it was as long as a school bus and had teeth as big as an adult man's hand.

Carcharocles megalodon was a huge shark with giant, serrated (jagged) teeth. It was much like today's great white shark, but even stronger. For a long time, it was thought to be a species of giant great white, but recent studies make scientists think that it is more closely related to mako sharks.

TEETH
The largest known teeth of this shark reached 8 in (20 cm) in length, but there were also much smaller ones in its mouth.

VERTEBRAE
Sometimes shark vertebrae harden enough during life that they can become fossils more easily. Known *C. megalodon* vertebrae are such examples.

HOW BIG IS IT?

TIMELINE (millions of years ago)

540	505	438	408	360	280	248	208	146	65	1.8 to today

Glossary

aerodynamic (eh-row-dy-NAM-ik) Relating to motion in the air; flight

ammonite (AH-muh-nite) An extinct cephalopod with a flat, spiral shell

bivalve (BY-valv) A type of marine mollusk with a two-piece hinged shell, such as a clam or oyster

camouflage (KAM-uh-flawj) To disguise by blending in with the surroundings

cavity (KA-vih-tee) A hollow space

digits (DIH-jits) Divisions of a limb, such as fingers

fossil (FAH-sil) Remains or traces of an organism from the past that have been preserved, such as bones, teeth, footprints, etc.

lagoon (luh-GOON) A shallow pond connected to a larger body of water

microfossil (my-kro-FAH-sil) A very small fossil that can only be studied under a microscope

paleontologist (pay-lee-on-TAH-luh-jist) A scientist who studies fossils

pampas (PAM-puz) Grass-covered plains

placodont (PLAK-oh-dont) A group of marine reptiles from the Triassic with flat, tough teeth to crush the shells of mollusks

shoal (SHOWL) A large group

wingspan (WING-span) The distance from the tip of one wing to the tip of the other wing

Index

46

For More Information

Books

Arnold, Caroline. *Giant Sea Reptiles of the Dinosaur Age.* New York: Clarion Books, 2007.

Collard, Sneed B. *Reign of the Sea Dragons.* Watertown, MA: Charlesbridge Publishing, 2008.

Gray, Susan Heinrichs. *Ichthyosaurs.* Mankato, MN: Child's World, 2005.

Web Sites

To ensure the currency and safety of recommended Internet links, Windmill maintains and updates an online list of sites related to the subject of this book. To access this list of Web sites, please go to www.windmillbooks.com/weblinks and select this book's title.

For more great fiction and nonfiction,
go to www.windmillbooks.com.